CW00658321

Blind Loyalty:

The Danger of Following Without Questioning

By

Troy D. Harris

DISCLAIMER

Copyright © by Troy D. Harris 2022. All rights reserved. Before this document is duplicated or reproduced in any manner, the publisher's consent must be gained. Therefore, the contents within can neither be stored electronically, transferred, nor kept in a database. Neither in Part nor full can the document be copied, scanned, faxed, or retained without approval from the publisher or creator.

TABLE OF CONTENT

INTRODUCTION

As human beings, we have an innate desire to belong and be accepted by others. We crave a sense of community and often seek out groups that share our values and beliefs. However, this desire for belonging can sometimes lead us down a dangerous path.

Blind loyalty is the act of following someone or something without questioning its validity or considering its potential consequences. It is a dangerous mindset that can lead individuals, groups, and even entire societies astray.

Throughout history, we have seen the devastating effects of blind loyalty. From the rise of dictators to the emergence of extremist groups, blind loyalty has been a driving force behind some of the world's most horrific atrocities.

We must understand the dangers of blind loyalty and the importance of questioning those we follow. By blindly following others, we relinquish our agency and allow ourselves to be manipulated by those who may not have our best interests at heart.

In this book, we will explore the various forms of blind loyalty and their consequences. We will examine the psychological and social factors that contribute to blind loyalty and how it can be identified and challenged.

We will also provide practical strategies for developing critical thinking skills and encouraging healthy scepticism. By learning to question and challenge our own beliefs and those of others, we can become more informed and independent thinkers.

This book is not just a book about the dangers of blind loyalty; it is a call to action. It is a reminder that we all have the power to question, challenge, and make informed decisions.

Blind loyalty can manifest in many different forms, from religious and political affiliations to personal relationships and even within the workplace. It is a complex issue that requires a deep understanding of human behaviour and the factors that influence our decision-making processes.

One of the most significant dangers of blind loyalty is the potential for groupthink. Groupthink is a phenomenon in which a group of individuals prioritises consensus and conformity over critical thinking and independent decision-making. This can lead to a dangerous echo chamber, in which dissenting voices are silenced, and the group becomes increasingly isolated from opposing viewpoints.

In such situations, individuals can become blinded by their loyalty to the group or leader, and they may overlook the negative consequences of their actions. This can result in unethical behaviour, harmful decision-making, and even violence.

Another danger of blind loyalty is the potential for manipulation by those in positions of power. Leaders who encourage blind loyalty may use fear, intimidation, or even rewards to maintain their followers' loyalty, despite their actions' negative consequences.

In such situations, followers may feel trapped or powerless, unsure of how to escape the cycle of loyalty and abuse. They may feel compelled to continue supporting their leader, despite evidence that they are harming themselves or others.

It is essential to recognize the signs of blind loyalty and the dangers it poses. By developing critical thinking skills, individuals can learn to question their own beliefs and the beliefs of those around them. They can become more independent and less susceptible to manipulation, enabling them to make informed decisions that align with their values and principles.

We will explore the factors that contribute to blind loyalty and provide practical strategies for overcoming them. We will examine case studies of individuals and groups who have fallen prey to blind loyalty and the consequences of their actions.

We will also explore the power of critical thinking, independent decision-making, and healthy scepticism. By learning to think for ourselves and challenge the status quo, we can become more empowered and effective in our personal and professional lives.

Blind loyalty is a dangerous mindset that can have far-reaching consequences for individuals, groups, and society as a whole. I hope that this book will raise awareness of this issue and inspire readers to become more independent, critical thinkers. By doing so, we can create a more just and equitable world, one that values individual agency and critical thinking over blind loyalty.

I hope that this book will inspire readers to question their own beliefs and the beliefs of those around them. That it will empower them to think critically and to stand up for what is right, even when it may be difficult. I believe that together, we can create a more informed and just society, one that values critical thinking and individual agency over blind loyalty.

Chapter 1

THE ILLUSION OF LOYALTY

Loyalty is often touted as a virtue, something to be valued and celebrated. We are taught to be loyal to our families, our friends, our communities, and our country. We are taught that loyalty is a sign of strength and character. But what happens when loyalty becomes blind, when it becomes a form of obedience and subservience rather than a genuine commitment to the people and ideals we hold dear? In this chapter, we explore the illusion of loyalty and how it can be dangerous.

The problem with blind loyalty is that it can lead to unquestioning obedience, even when that obedience goes against our values and principles. Blind loyalty can lead us to ignore or even defend wrongdoing, simply because it is being committed by someone we are loyal to. Blind loyalty can also lead us to overlook the flaws and failings of those we are loyal to, allowing them to continue making mistakes or engaging in harmful behaviour without any accountability.

One example of blind loyalty in action is the phenomenon of cults. Cults are often characterised by a group of people who are loyal to a charismatic leader or set of ideas. Cult members are often willing to go to extreme lengths to please their leader, even if it means engaging in harmful or illegal behaviour. The blind loyalty of cult members can be so strong that it can be difficult to break free from the group, even when it becomes clear that the leader or the group's ideas are harmful.

Another example of the illusion of loyalty can be found in political or ideological movements. When people become attached to a particular political ideology or party, they can become blind to its flaws and failings. They may ignore or even defend actions or policies that are harmful or unethical, simply because they are loyal to their party or ideology. This type of blind loyalty can be especially dangerous in a democracy, where dissent and criticism are essential for holding those in power accountable.

The illusion of loyalty can also be found in more everyday situations, such as in the workplace. Employees who are blindly loyal to their bosses or their company may overlook or even participate in unethical behaviour simply because they feel a sense of loyalty to the organisation. This type of blind loyalty can create a toxic work environment, where people are afraid to speak out against wrongdoing or challenge the status quo.

So how do we avoid the illusion of loyalty and ensure that our loyalty is genuine and based on our values and principles? One important step is to cultivate a sense of independence and critical thinking. We must be willing to question authority and challenge ideas and actions that go against our values, even if it means going against those we are loyal to. We must also be willing to hold ourselves and those we are loyal to accountable for their actions, and to be open to criticism and feedback.

Another important step is to cultivate a sense of empathy and compassion. Blind loyalty often comes from a sense of attachment or belonging, but true loyalty should be based on a genuine concern for the well-being of others. We must be willing to put the interests of others above our self-interest and to act with kindness and compassion even when it is difficult or inconvenient.

Ultimately, the illusion of loyalty is dangerous because it can lead us to become blind to the harm we are causing or enabling. We must strive to cultivate a sense of genuine loyalty that is based on our values, our principles, and our concern for the well-being of others. We must be willing to question authority and challenge ideas and actions that go against these values, even if it means going against those we are loyal to. Only then can we truly live up to the virtue of loyalty, and avoid the dangers of blind obedience and subservience?

To further avoid the illusion of loyalty, we must also be willing to listen to and learn from those who hold different perspectives or opinions. Blind loyalty can often be the result of surrounding ourselves with people who only reinforce our beliefs and opinions, leading us to dismiss or ignore those who hold different views. By engaging in respectful dialogue and seeking out diverse perspectives, we can challenge our own beliefs and ensure that our loyalty is based on a deep understanding of the world around us.

It's also important to recognize that loyalty is not a one-way street. Loyalty is a two-way commitment, and those we are loyal to must also demonstrate a commitment to our well-being and to the values we share. If someone we are loyal to consistently engages in harmful or unethical behaviour, it may be time to reevaluate our loyalty and consider whether it is truly genuine or whether it has become a form of blind obedience.

In some cases, it may be necessary to break ties with those we are loyal to if they are engaging in harmful behaviour that goes against our values and principles. While this can be a difficult and painful decision, it is sometimes necessary to ensure that our loyalty is based on our genuine commitment to the well-being of others.

The illusion of loyalty can be dangerous and can lead us down a path of blind obedience and subservience. To avoid this, we must cultivate a sense of independence, critical thinking, empathy, and compassion. We must be willing to question authority and challenge ideas and actions that go against our values, and we must be open to learning from diverse perspectives. By doing so, we can ensure that our loyalty is genuine and based on a deep commitment to the well-being of others. Only then can we avoid the dangers of blind loyalty and live up to the true virtues of loyalty and commitment

Chapter 2

THE PSYCHOLOGY
OF BLIND LOYALTY

Blind loyalty is a topic that has fascinated psychologists, sociologists, and other social scientists for decades. It is a phenomenon where individuals are willing to follow a group or a leader without questioning their actions or beliefs. Blind loyalty can be dangerous as it can lead to groupthink, conformity, and a lack of critical thinking. In this chapter, we will explore the psychology of blind loyalty and its potential consequences.

The concept of blind loyalty can be traced back to the early work of social psychologist Solomon Asch. Asch's conformity experiments in the 1950s showed how individuals can be influenced by a group to conform to the group's beliefs or actions, even if they know that those beliefs or actions are wrong. Asch's work highlighted the importance of social pressure and the fear of being rejected by the group in shaping an individual's behaviour.

Blind loyalty is closely related to groupthink, a phenomenon that occurs when a group of individuals prioritises harmony and agreement over critical thinking and independent judgement. Groupthink can occur in a variety of settings, such as corporations, political organisations, and religious groups. When groupthink takes hold, dissenting opinions are discouraged or even punished, and group members may feel pressure to conform to the majority opinion.

One of the key drivers of blind loyalty is the need for social belonging. Humans are social animals, and we have a fundamental need to feel accepted and valued by our peers. This need can be so strong that we are willing to compromise our values and beliefs to fit in with the group. As a result, individuals who feel a strong sense of social identity may be more susceptible to blind loyalty.

Another factor that can contribute to blind loyalty is the tendency to defer to authority figures. This is often seen in hierarchical organisations, such as the military or police force, where individuals are expected to follow orders without question. In these settings, individuals may feel a sense of duty or obligation to the organisation, which can override their judgement and critical thinking abilities.

The consequences of blind loyalty can be severe. In extreme cases, blind loyalty can lead to acts of violence, such as terrorist attacks or cult suicides. However, even in less extreme cases, blind loyalty can lead to poor decision-making and a lack of accountability. When individuals are unwilling to question their leaders or the group's actions, it can create a culture of silence and complacency, which can be detrimental to the organisation or society as a whole.

One of the most famous examples of blind loyalty in recent history is the Jonestown Massacre. In 1978, cult leader Jim Jones led more than 900 of his followers to commit mass suicide in Guyana. Jones had convinced his followers that they were under threat from the outside world and that suicide was the only way to avoid persecution. The tragedy highlighted the dangers of blind loyalty and the power of the charismatic leader to manipulate and control their followers.

To prevent blind loyalty, it is important to encourage critical thinking and independent judgement. This can be achieved by promoting a culture of open communication and encouraging individuals to voice their opinions and concerns. Leaders should be willing to listen to dissenting opinions and be open to feedback and constructive criticism. In addition, organisations should promote diversity and inclusion, which can help to reduce the effects of groupthink and encourage a wider range of perspectives and ideas.

Furthermore, education can play a significant role in preventing blind loyalty. Educating individuals about the dangers of blind loyalty and the importance of critical thinking can help individuals recognize the signs of groupthink and blind loyalty in themselves and others. This can include teaching individuals about bias, confirmation bias, and logical fallacies.

Another important factor is the cultivation of empathy and compassion. Blind loyalty can often arise from a sense of an "us vs. them" mentality, where individuals see themselves as part of an exclusive group that is superior to others. By promoting empathy and compassion, individuals can recognize the commonalities they share with others and avoid falling into the trap of blind loyalty. It is also important to note that blind loyalty is not always a negative phenomenon. Blind loyalty can be a positive force when it is directed towards ethical, moral, and just causes. Blind loyalty to a cause that is rooted in social justice, human rights, and the betterment of society can lead to positive change. However, blind loyalty can become problematic when it is directed toward individuals or groups that promote harmful, discriminatory, or unethical practices.

Blind loyalty is a complex phenomenon that has the potential to cause harm. It is driven by a need for social belonging and the tendency to defer to authority figures. To prevent blind loyalty, it is important to encourage critical thinking and independent judgement, promote open communication, value diversity and inclusion, educate individuals, cultivate empathy and compassion, and ensure that blind loyalty is directed towards ethical, moral, and just causes. By doing so, we can build stronger, more resilient organisations and societies that promote positive change and improve the lives of individuals around the world. We can also create organisations and societies that are more resilient, adaptive, and accountable.

Chapter 3

THE CONSEQUENCE OF BLIND LOYALTY

Blind loyalty can have disastrous consequences for individuals. When we blindly follow someone or something, we give up our critical thinking and ability to make informed decisions. This can lead to us making choices that go against our values, beliefs, and even our well-being.

For example, a person who is blindly loyal to a religious leader may be convinced to engage in harmful practices, such as self-harm or sacrificing their interests for the sake of the group. Similarly, a person who blindly follows a political leader may support policies that go against their best interests or those of society.

In extreme cases, blind loyalty can lead to violence and even death. We have seen examples of this throughout history, where people have committed atrocities in the name of their leaders or ideologies.

Blind loyalty can also have severe consequences for organisations. When people within an organisation blindly follow a leader, it can lead to groupthink, where individuals stop questioning decisions and ideas. This can stifle creativity and innovation, leading to a stagnant organisation that fails to adapt to changing circumstances.

Furthermore, when people blindly follow a leader, they may be reluctant to speak out about issues or problems within the organisation. This can lead to a toxic culture where problems go unaddressed, leading to a decline in productivity, morale, and ultimately, the demise of the organisation.

Blind loyalty can have even more severe consequences for society as a whole. When a significant portion of society blindly follows a leader or ideology, it can lead to polarisation and division. People may become unwilling to listen to opposing viewpoints or engage in constructive dialogue, leading to conflict and even violence.

Furthermore, blind loyalty can lead to the erosion of democracy and the rule of law. When people blindly follow a leader, they may be willing to overlook or even condone actions that go against the principles of democracy, such as the suppression of free speech, the press, and human rights.

Why Do People Fall Into the Trap of Blind Loyalty?

There are several reasons why people fall into the trap of blind loyalty. One of the most common is a desire for certainty and stability. When we are faced with uncertainty and ambiguity, we may feel anxious and insecure. Blindly following a leader or ideology can provide a sense of certainty and stability, even if it is false.

Another reason people fall into the trap of blind loyalty is a desire for belonging and acceptance. We all want to feel like we belong to a group, and blindly following a leader or ideology can provide us with a sense of belonging and acceptance. However, this sense of belonging often comes at the cost of our individuality and critical thinking.

What Can Be Done to Avoid Blind Loyalty?
The first step in avoiding blind loyalty is to recognize its dangers. We need to understand that blindly following a leader or ideology can have severe consequences for ourselves, organisations, and society as a whole. We need to cultivate our critical thinking skills and learn to question decisions and ideas, even if they come from a respected authority figure.

We also need to be aware of our own biases and the influence of groupthink. We should seek out diverse viewpoints and engage in constructive dialogue with those who hold different opinions. By exposing ourselves to different ideas and perspectives, we can broaden our understanding of the world and make more informed decisions.

Another way to avoid blind loyalty is to cultivate a sense of individuality and independence. We should be comfortable with our own beliefs and values and not be afraid to stand up for what we believe in, even if it goes against the group or authority figure.

Finally, we should seek out leaders and organisations that value transparency, accountability, and open communication. When we have leaders who encourage questioning and dissent, it can lead to a more innovative and adaptive organisation or society.

Blind loyalty can have severe consequences, both for individuals and society as a whole. When we blindly follow someone or something, we give up our critical thinking and ability to make informed decisions. This can lead to choices that go against our values, beliefs, and well-being, and even result in violence and death.

To avoid blind loyalty, we need to cultivate our critical thinking skills, be aware of our biases, and seek out diverse viewpoints. We should also value individuality and independence and seek out leaders and organisations that encourage transparency, accountability, and open communication.

Blind loyalty is a dangerous trap that we must all be aware of and avoid. By doing so, we can create a more just, equitable, and sustainable society for ourselves and future generations.

Chapter 4

RECOGNIZING BLIND LOYALTY

Blind Loyalty is a phenomenon that has been prevalent in many cultures, organisations, and societies throughout history. It involves people adhering to a certain belief, idea, or leader without questioning its validity or morality. This behaviour can lead to dangerous outcomes, as people who blindly follow may be susceptible to manipulation, abuse, and even violence. In this chapter, we will explore the concept of recognizing blind loyalty, its dangers, and how to avoid falling into this trap.

Blind loyalty is often associated with cults or extremist groups. These organisations create a sense of community and belonging by convincing their members that they are the only ones who have the truth. They manipulate their followers by using fear, guilt, and shame to prevent them from questioning their beliefs or the actions of their leaders. This kind of loyalty can result in the members being subjected to physical or emotional abuse, or even being coerced into committing illegal or immoral acts.

However, blind loyalty is not only present in cults or extremist groups. It can also be found in everyday situations, such as in relationships, workplaces, or politics. People may blindly follow their partners, bosses, or political leaders without questioning their motives or actions. This kind of loyalty can result in unhealthy relationships, workplace toxicity, and even corruption in government.

One of the most significant dangers of blind loyalty is the inability to recognize when one is being manipulated. When a person is blindly loyal to a certain idea or leader, they are more likely to dismiss or ignore any evidence or criticism that goes against their beliefs. They become closed-minded and unwilling to consider any other perspective, which can lead to a lack of critical thinking and a failure to recognize when they are being manipulated.

Therefore, it is crucial to recognize the signs of blind loyalty. These signs include a lack of critical thinking, an unwillingness to consider other perspectives, a tendency to dismiss or ignore evidence or criticism, and an irrational devotion to an idea or leader. When people are blindly loyal, they often become defensive when their beliefs or leaders are challenged, and they may resort to personal attacks or other aggressive behaviour to defend their position.

To avoid falling into the trap of blind loyalty, it is essential to develop critical thinking skills and be willing to question everything. People should ask themselves why they believe what they do, and they should be open to considering other perspectives. They should also research and gather evidence to support their beliefs and be willing to change their minds if new information arises. Moreover, it is important to be aware of manipulative tactics used by leaders or organisations and to recognize when they are being used.

It is important to note that blind loyalty is not always a negative thing. In certain situations, loyalty can be a positive trait. For example, in friendships, loyalty is a key component of trust and can create a strong bond between individuals. However, blind loyalty should never be prioritised over critical thinking and consideration of evidence and opposing perspectives.

Recognizing blind loyalty is not always easy, as it often manifests itself in subtle ways. One way to spot it is by paying attention to the language used by individuals or groups. For example, they may use language that creates a sense of "us versus them," or they may dismiss opposing views as being misguided or ignorant. Another sign is when individuals or groups rely heavily on emotions and feelings rather than rational thinking and evidence-based arguments.

To avoid falling into the trap of blind loyalty, individuals should practise mindfulness and self-awareness. This involves reflecting on one's own beliefs and values, as well as being aware of one's own biases and limitations. Additionally, individuals should be willing to seek out and consider feedback and criticism from others, as well as engage in respectful and constructive dialogue with individuals who hold opposing views.

One effective way to recognize blind loyalty is to look for red flags or warning signs. For example, if a leader or organisation is unwilling to answer questions or provide evidence to support their claims, this may indicate that they are relying on blind loyalty rather than rational thinking and evidence-based arguments. Additionally, if an individual or group is overly defensive or aggressive when their beliefs or actions are challenged, this may also be a sign of blind loyalty.

Blind loyalty can be a dangerous and destructive behaviour that can lead to manipulation, abuse, and even violence. Recognizing the signs of blind loyalty is essential in avoiding this trap, and it is important to develop critical thinking skills and be willing to question everything. By doing so, individuals can avoid becoming victims of blind loyalty and become more empowered in their decision-making processes. It is important to remember that loyalty can be a positive trait, but it should never be prioritised over critical thinking and consideration of evidence and opposing perspectives

Chapter 5

BREAKING FREE
FROM BLIND
LOYALTY

Blind loyalty can be defined as an unwavering commitment to a person, group, or ideology, without questioning their motives or actions. This type of loyalty can be dangerous because it can lead to individuals blindly following their leaders, without thinking critically about the consequences of their actions.

Breaking free from blind loyalty requires individuals to develop critical thinking skills, question authority, and take responsibility for their own beliefs and actions. It is important to recognize the signs of blind loyalty and understand how it can be detrimental to personal and societal growth.

One of the main dangers of blind loyalty is that it can lead to individuals blindly following their leaders, without thinking critically about the consequences of their actions. This can be seen in cults, where members blindly follow their leaders, even if it means committing heinous acts. It can also be seen in political movements, where individuals blindly follow a party or ideology, without questioning the policies or actions of their leaders.

Blind loyalty can also lead to individuals overlooking the flaws of their leaders and failing to hold them accountable for their actions. This can result in leaders abusing their power, engaging in corrupt practices, and making decisions that are not in the best interest of their followers.

To break free from blind loyalty, individuals must develop critical thinking skills. This involves questioning authority, challenging assumptions, and seeking out information from multiple sources. It also requires individuals to be open-minded and willing to consider alternative perspectives.

Another important step in breaking free from blind loyalty is taking responsibility for one's own beliefs and actions. This involves recognizing the role that personal biases and emotions play in shaping beliefs and opinions and taking steps to mitigate their influence. It also involves being accountable for the consequences of one's actions and decisions, rather than blindly following the directives of others.

Breaking free from blind loyalty can be a difficult and sometimes painful process. It may require individuals to confront uncomfortable truths and challenge deeply held beliefs. It may also involve facing criticism and opposition from those who are still committed to blind loyalty.

However, the benefits of breaking free from blind loyalty are significant. It allows individuals to think for themselves, make informed decisions, and take responsibility for their own lives. It also promotes personal growth and development and can lead to a more just and equitable society.

Additionally, breaking free from blind loyalty can lead to a greater sense of individual freedom and empowerment. When individuals can think for themselves and make their own decisions, they are less likely to be controlled by outside forces. This can prompt a more prominent feeling of independence and self-assurance.

Furthermore, breaking free from blind loyalty can lead to a more diverse and inclusive society. When individuals are encouraged to question authority and challenge assumptions, they are more likely to seek out alternative perspectives and consider the experiences of others. This can lead to a greater understanding and appreciation of different cultures, beliefs, and lifestyles.

However, breaking free from blind loyalty can also be challenging. It can be difficult to overcome the influence of group dynamics and social pressure. Individuals may face backlash from their peers or community for questioning authority or challenging the status quo.

To overcome these challenges, individuals need to seek out support from like-minded individuals or groups. This can provide a sense of community and validation for those who are breaking free from blind loyalty. It is also important for individuals to take care of their mental health and well-being during this process, as it can be emotionally draining and stressful.

Blind loyalty can be dangerous because it can lead to individuals blindly following their leaders, without thinking critically about the consequences of their actions. Breaking free from blind loyalty requires individuals to develop critical thinking skills, question authority, and take responsibility for their own beliefs and actions. While it can be a difficult process, breaking free from blind loyalty is essential for personal and societal growth.

Breaking free from blind loyalty is an essential step toward personal and societal growth. It requires individuals to develop critical thinking skills, question authority, and take responsibility for their own beliefs and actions - We will be discussing Critical thinking in the next chapter. While it can be a challenging process, breaking free from blind loyalty can lead to greater individual freedom, diversity, and inclusion. Individuals need to seek out support and prioritise their mental health during this process.

Chapter 6

THE BENEFITS OF CRITICAL THINKING

Blind loyalty can be dangerous. When we blindly follow someone or something without questioning, we can be led astray, whether it's in our relationships, our careers, or our political beliefs. Blind loyalty can cause us to make poor decisions and act in ways that are detrimental to our interests and those of others.

Critical thinking is the antidote to blind loyalty. It involves questioning, analysing, and evaluating information and ideas systematically and logically. When we engage in critical thinking, we can make informed decisions and act in ways that are consistent with our values and beliefs.

We will explore the benefits of critical thinking and how it can help us avoid the pitfalls of blind loyalty.

Improved Decision-Making
One of the most significant benefits of critical thinking is improved decision-making. When we engage in critical thinking, we can weigh the pros and cons of different options and make decisions that are based on logic and evidence rather than emotion or blind loyalty.

For instance, suppose that you are thinking about purchasing another vehicle. If you engage in critical thinking, you will research different car models, compare prices and features, and consider factors such as fuel efficiency and safety ratings. Based on this analysis, you will be able to make an informed decision about which car to buy.

On the other hand, if you blindly follow the advice of a car salesman without doing your research, you may end up buying a car that is not right for you and that you later regret.

Better Problem-Solving

Another benefit of critical thinking is better problem-solving. When we encounter a problem, critical thinking helps us to break it down into its parts and to analyse each part in detail. By doing so, we can identify the root cause of the problem and develop effective solutions.

For example, let's say that you are having trouble with a coworker who is consistently late with their work. If you engage in critical thinking, you will identify the specific behaviours that are causing the problem, such as missed deadlines or poor communication. You will then develop a plan of action to address these behaviours and to improve your working relationship with your coworker.

Without critical thinking, you may simply become frustrated with your coworker and blame them for the problem without addressing the underlying issues.

Enhanced Creativity
Contrary to popular belief, critical thinking is not just about analysing and evaluating information. It also involves creative thinking and problem-solving. When we engage in critical thinking, we can think outside the box and come up with innovative solutions to problems.

For example, let's say that you are tasked with coming up with a new marketing campaign for your company. If you engage in critical thinking, you will not only analyse the current market trends and consumer behaviour, but you will also think creatively about how to reach your target audience in new and innovative ways.

By doing so, you may come up with a marketing campaign that is more effective and impactful than anything your competitors have done.

Improved Communication Skills
Critical thinking also enhances our communication skills. When we engage in critical thinking, we can

clearly articulate our ideas and communicate them in a way that is logical, persuasive, and easy to understand.

For example, let's say that you are presenting a proposal to your boss. If you engage in critical thinking, you will be able to clearly explain your proposal, provide evidence to support your claims, and address any potential objections or concerns that your boss may have.

Without critical thinking, you may struggle to articulate your ideas and persuade others to see things from your perspective.

Blind loyalty can be dangerous, and it can lead us down a path that is not in our best interests. Critical thinking, on the other hand, provides us with a framework for making informed decisions and taking thoughtful action.

We have explored some of the key benefits of critical thinking, including improved decision-making, better problem-solving, enhanced creativity, and improved communication skills. By engaging in critical thinking, we can approach challenges and opportunities with a clear and rational mindset, free from the biases and limitations that can come from blind loyalty.

As we continue to explore the dangers of blind loyalty in this book, we will return to the theme of critical thinking and its role in helping us to navigate the complex and the often unpredictable world around us. Whether we are making decisions in our personal lives, our professional careers, or our political beliefs, critical thinking is an essential tool for ensuring that we stay true to our values and make choices that are in our best interests and the interests of those around us.

By understanding the underlying motivations and pressures that can lead us down this path, we can begin to develop the critical thinking skills that are necessary for breaking free from blind loyalty and making choices that are truly our own.

Chapter 7

BUILDING HEALTHY RELATIONSHIPS

In a world where loyalty is often valued above all else, blind loyalty can be a dangerous force. Blind loyalty is the act of following someone or something without question, even when it goes against one's own beliefs or values. It can lead to destructive relationships and even harmful actions. However, building healthy relationships can be the antidote to blind loyalty.

Solid relationships depend on common regard, trust, and correspondence. They are built on a foundation of shared values and goals. They allow individuals to grow and develop while also supporting one another. In healthy relationships, individuals are encouraged to think for themselves and make their own decisions. This can help prevent blind loyalty from taking hold.

One of the keys to building healthy relationships is communication. Listening is at the core of powerful correspondence. It requires individuals to be open and honest with one another, even when it's difficult. It also involves actively trying to understand the other person's perspective. By communicating effectively, individuals can build trust and respect with one another.

Another key to building healthy relationships is setting boundaries. Boundaries are the limits individuals set for themselves in terms of what they are willing to accept from others. They can include things like how much time they are willing to spend with someone or what topics they are comfortable discussing. By setting boundaries, individuals can protect their well-being and ensure that their needs are being met.

In addition to communication and setting boundaries, building healthy relationships requires a willingness to compromise. Compromise involves finding a middle ground that both parties can agree on. It requires individuals to be flexible and willing to consider alternative solutions. By compromising, individuals can find solutions that work for everyone involved.

Another important aspect of building healthy relationships is recognizing and addressing issues as they arise. Conflict is a natural part of any relationship, but it's how individuals handle conflict that can determine whether a relationship is healthy or not. Healthy relationships involve addressing issues as they arise, rather than avoiding them or letting them fester. This requires individuals to be willing to confront issues head-on and work toward a resolution.

Building healthy relationships also involves recognizing and valuing diversity. Everyone has different experiences and perspectives, and healthy relationships involve respecting and appreciating those differences. By valuing diversity, individuals can learn from one another and grow together.

Finally, building healthy relationships involves taking care of oneself. Taking care of oneself is the demonstration of dealing with one's physical, close-to-home, and mental prosperity. It's important to prioritise self-care in any relationship, as individuals who neglect their own needs may become resentful or burned out. By taking care of themselves, individuals can show up fully in their relationships and be present for others.

Moreover, healthy relationships can also help individuals to overcome the negative consequences of blind loyalty. When individuals blindly follow someone or something, they may become trapped in a toxic environment where they are unable to grow and develop as a person. They may also become disconnected from their own beliefs and values, leading to a loss of identity and purpose.

However, by building healthy relationships, individuals can regain their sense of self and break free from the constraints of blind loyalty. Healthy relationships allow individuals to develop their own opinions and beliefs, without fear of judgement or rejection. They provide a safe space where individuals can express themselves freely and receive support and encouragement.

In addition, healthy relationships can also provide individuals with a sense of belonging and community. Blind loyalty can often lead to a sense of isolation and disconnection from others, as individuals may feel unable to connect with people who do not share their beliefs or values. However, healthy relationships provide a sense of belonging and connectedness, as individuals can connect with others who share their values and goals.

Furthermore, healthy relationships can also help individuals to develop their interpersonal skills. When individuals blindly follow someone or something, they may lack the confidence and skills to form healthy relationships with others. However, by building healthy relationships, individuals can develop their communication, conflict resolution, and empathy skills. These skills can be applied not only in personal relationships but also in professional and social contexts.

Building healthy relationships is the antidote to blind loyalty. Blind loyalty can be a dangerous force that leads to toxic relationships and a loss of identity and purpose. However, by building healthy relationships based on mutual respect, trust, and communication, individuals can prevent blind loyalty from taking hold and cultivate relationships that support their growth and well-being. Healthy relationships provide individuals with a sense of belonging, community, and connectedness, and help them to develop their interpersonal skills. By prioritising healthy relationships, individuals can break free from the negative consequences of blind loyalty and live a more fulfilling and authentic life.

Chapter 8

CONCLUSION

The book Blind Loyalty: The Danger of Following Without Questioning is a powerful exploration of the perils of blindly following authority figures or organisations without critically examining their actions or motives. Throughout the book, we have seen numerous examples of the disastrous consequences that can result when individuals or groups put loyalty above reason and blindly accept what they are told without questioning its validity.

One of the central themes of the book is the importance of critical thinking. Blindly following authority figures or organisations without questioning their actions or motives is dangerous because it leaves us vulnerable to manipulation and exploitation. To avoid falling into this trap, we must cultivate our critical thinking skills and be willing to question what we are told.

Another important lesson from the book is the need to be aware of our own biases and prejudices. Blind loyalty often arises when we feel a strong emotional connection to an individual or group, or when we share their values or beliefs. This emotional attachment can blind us to the flaws and shortcomings of those we follow, and can prevent us from seeing the truth when it contradicts our preconceived notions. By being aware of our own biases and prejudices, we can take steps to overcome them and make more informed decisions.

A related theme in the book is the importance of seeking out diverse perspectives and opinions. Blind loyalty often arises when we are surrounded by others who share our beliefs and values, creating an echo chamber in which dissenting voices are silenced. By seeking out a variety of viewpoints, we can expose ourselves to new ideas and challenge our assumptions. This can help us avoid the trap of blind loyalty and make more informed decisions.

The dangers of blind loyalty are not limited to political or religious organisations. The book has also explored the dangers of blind loyalty in corporate environments, where employees may feel pressure to follow orders from their superiors even when those orders are unethical or illegal. To avoid falling into this trap, it is important to cultivate a strong sense of ethics and integrity and to be willing to speak out when we see something that is wrong.

Throughout the book, we have seen numerous examples of the disastrous consequences that can result when blind loyalty goes unchecked. From the rise of authoritarian regimes to the corporate scandals that have rocked the business world, blind loyalty has played a role in some of the darkest moments in human history. By understanding the dangers of blind loyalty, we can take steps to avoid falling into this trap ourselves and work to build a more just and equitable world.

It is important to note that avoiding blind loyalty is not easy. We are all susceptible to the lure of charismatic leaders or organisations that promise to solve our problems or provide us with a sense of belonging. However, by understanding the dangers of blind loyalty and taking steps to mitigate them, we can reduce the risk of falling into this trap.

One of the most effective ways to avoid blind loyalty is to cultivate a strong sense of individualism. This means valuing our thoughts and opinions, even if they go against the prevailing wisdom of the group. It also means being willing to take risks and stand up for what we believe in, even when it is unpopular. By valuing our individuality, we can avoid the trap of blindly following others and making decisions that are true to our values and beliefs.

Another important factor in avoiding blind loyalty is building strong social networks. Having a diverse group of friends and colleagues who challenge us and offer different perspectives can help us avoid falling into echo chambers where we only hear the opinions of those who share our views. Additionally, being part of a community can provide us with a sense of belonging and purpose without requiring us to surrender our critical thinking skills.

Finally, we must be willing to hold those in positions of power accountable for their actions. This means speaking out when we see injustice or corruption, and holding leaders accountable for their actions. We must also be willing to take action ourselves, whether through activism, voting, or other means of engaging with the world around us.

This book is a powerful reminder of the importance of critical thinking, self-awareness, and a willingness to challenge authority. The dangers of blind loyalty are all around us, from politics to business to our personal lives. By staying vigilant and being willing to question what we are told, we can avoid falling into this trap and make more informed decisions. As we move forward, we hope that this book will inspire readers to take action and build a more just and equitable world.

Printed in Great Britain
by Amazon

41189740R00036